WORKING WISDOM

WORKING WISDOM

A Guide to the Art and Strategy of Success at Work

Patricia Monaghan

HarperSanFrancisco
A Division of HarperCollins*Publishers*

For information address HarperCollins Publishers, 10 East 53rd Street, New York, NY 10022.

FIRST EDITION

Library of Congress Cataloging-in-Publication Data

Monaghan, Patricia

Working wisdom : a guide to the art and strategy of success at work / Patricia Monaghan. — 1st ed.

p. cm.

ISBN 0-06-251074-6 (cloth).

ISBN 0-06-251084-3 (pbk.)

1. Quality of work life—Quotations, maxims, etc. 2. Interpersonal relations—Quotations, maxims, etc. I. Title.

HD6955.M62 1994

650.1—dc20 94-558 CIP

94 95 96 97 98 ❖ ARC(F) 10 9 8 7 6 5 4 3 2 1

This edition is printed on acid-free paper that meets the American National Standards Institute Z39.48 Standard.

To Jim Roginski

INTRODUCTION

Most mornings, we rise and go to work.

We spend our days there, sometimes our evenings as well. We meet friends and lovers there. We laugh there, and sometimes we cry.

We find ourselves in our work; often we lose ourselves in it. We are hurt there, and there we recover. We learn there, grow there, change there.

This is the way our lives are now. This is the way they will be for all our working years.

It is easy to spend these precious hours like common coins, not recognizing their value. It is easy to pass through our working days asleep to their transformative potential. But to live fully, we must live consciously at all times—at work, as well as at play or at prayer. We must be always in touch with our souls, with our selves.

Some claim that worldly work opposes or degrades the soul. Do you wish to live nobly? Live on a mountaintop, they say. Do you wish to commune with the light? Retreat to the forest, they say. Do you wish to find peace? Hide in the trackless desert, they tell us.

But on the mountaintop, there are no people to inspire. In the forest depths, there is no one to lead. In the desert, there is no one to teach. And if some find salvation in retreat from the world, others discover their souls in engagement with it.

Setting is no guarantee of the presence of spirituality—nor any proof of its absence. Nobility and communion are as difficult to attain on a mountaintop as in a meeting. It is just as possible to lose one's soul on an island as in an industrial park. It is our daily choices that define our souls—not the location in which those choices are made.

Often we are not encouraged to bring our whole selves into the workplace. And so we leave our souls at home. We pass our days separated from our spiritual essence. Our search for meaning, our search for wisdom, we save for evenings, for weekends, for vacations.

A split develops in the soul that finds no meaning in its work. Yet this split need not occur. For even when we are unaware of it, the workplace is a place of spirit, a soulful place. It is a place of transformation.

The transformation begins with money. The bald fact is, we work for money. We may also work for prestige and fulfillment, of course. But money defines work: what is unpaid is volunteer service, a hobby, sport, or pleasure. Work is what we are paid to do.

Thus, to understand the spiritual meaning of work, we must understand that money serves as both symbol and agent of change. On the simplest level, we continually transform our time, our effort, our ideas into money. Then we work the magic of transformation again, turning money into food, shelter, clothing, and luxuries.

On an esoteric plane, the transformation of human effort into money represents the power of change. More mundanely, money offers the opportunity to alter our worlds. The presence or absence of money changes us. Those with little money often have little hope of transforming their lives. Those with much can do much.

Just as money has a spiritual meaning, so does success and power. Worldly success is often said to corrode the spirit. That can, of course, be true. But it need not be so. Success and power are not, in themselves, either positive or negative. It is what people choose to do with their power that affects the world for better or worse. But success gives them the power to choose—and the challenge to choose well.

Many other transformations reveal themselves to you at work. In any office, any market, any factory, there are hundreds of psychological, moral, ethical transformations daily. They occur even when you are oblivious to them. If you choose, you can grow aware of them and of their potential for life-shaking change. Most people, when they arrive at work, fall into a deep sleep. In a dreamlike trance they perform their duties, never seeing the potential for personal transformation that each task promises. They may befriend us or work against us, but always as though they are dreaming and we are part of their dream. When they move to another state, another job, they leave nothing behind to show what they have transformed.

Others, however, are awake. They are awake to the choices that continually confront them. Once we have awakened too, we can see them: they are the ones who, like yeasted bread, are rising. They too may befriend us or work against us, but these mentors or enemies transform our own awareness. They gain power and prestige; they make change happen; they create spaces that never existed. They are the wise ones of the workplace.

To become one of them, we must learn their secret: that all work partakes of wisdom. The wise ones are those who know how to observe and direct the transformation inherent in every change. Every wise worker is an alchemist, creating the new, the extraordinary, from the old and the ordinary.

You too can become a workplace alchemist. You can refuse to sleep through the marvelous flow and flux that surrounds you. You can open your eyes to the multiple possibilities of every occasion. You can learn to detect change as it is about to occur and use it to your advantage.

You can become one of the wise.

We are using our wisdom any time we use a symbolic system to tap into personal power. The power of symbols frees the spontaneous, powerful spirit within us. It permits us to apply our own deepest wisdom to whatever is at hand.

This book's oracles—a symbolic system to help you in attuning to your inner power—will not themselves guide you. But they will permit you to guide yourself.

The oracles will help you tune into the agent of change within you. We all know more than we consciously realize. Intuitions and lightning perceptions occur beyond the reach of normal thought. An oracle system such as this one channels the information you already have within you into a message that your conscious mind can hear.

You, in fact, have the answers already. But these oracles will help you articulate them to yourself. They will help you find the path when you believe you have lost it. They will help you use change to your benefit and that of others.

Use your inner knowledge wisely, and you will become successful and happy, powerful and respected. You will grow in influence and security. You will become one of those awake to the possibilities for positive change inherent in each moment.

For the point of wisdom is not simply to do well—it is also to do good. The world is waiting for you. You need only begin.

THE ORACULAR SYSTEM

To use this oracle, you will need four coins, two each of two different types. You may use unusual or antique coins, or you may just reach into your pocket for spare change. Any type of coins will do, as long as you have two pairs of identical coins.

Determine which pair of coins will be primary, which secondary. It is necessary to keep this consistent throughout the divination.

Money, used in commerce, is especially suitable to an oracle designed for use at work. Coins are readily available and rather inconspicuous, especially in the workplace. But there is a more important, symbolic reason for the choice of coins as oracle markers. To the dreaming mind, money represents change, especially the transformation of energy into product. We call coins "change" even today. Because of money's symbolic meaning, it is especially appropriate that you use coins to read your oracle herein.

Having selected your coins, you are ready to use them to determine which oracle will speak to you. You may, if you choose, ask a specific question or pose a specific problem to be addressed. Or you may simply put your mind in a meditative state and seek help of a general nature. In either case, it is important to be silent for a few moments before casting the coins in order to attune yourself to your inner wisdom.

There are four easy steps to follow in casting the oracle.

1. Cast the coins to determine the first number. Use this chart to determine which number will be in first place:

All heads or all tails	0
Two heads, two tails	1
Three heads, one tail or Three tails, one head	0

2. Cast the coins a second and a third time, determining their worth according to the following chart.

Primary Pair	*Secondary Pair*	*Number*
All tails		0
All heads		1
1 head, 1 tail	1 head, 1 tail	2
1 head, 1 tail	2 heads	3
1 head, 1 tail	2 tails	4
2 heads	1 head, 1 tail	5
2 tails	1 head, 1 tail	6
2 heads	2 tails	7
2 tails	2 heads	8

If you are interrupted in any way during either your second or third cast, write *nine* in that space. Interruptions can include telephone calls, visitors, or other external events. Or they can be internal to the oracular system: if a coin flies off the desk or rolls onto the floor, that number is nine.

Finally, if you throw four tails in each space, resulting in three zeros, your oracle number is 200.

3. Upon determining your oracle number, your next step will be to read the aphorism and its interpretation. Be sure to do so in a meditative way, looking for the wisdom it evokes within you. Ultimately, this oracle or any other is only as effective as you make it. Be open to all the possibilities the oracle indicates.

4. Your final step: go forth and put it to use!

THE ORACLES

1 ~ *It is easier to ask forgiveness than permission.*

Why wait for approval? It is too easy to find excuses to avoid action. Seeking approval may lead to long delays while others find reasons to object to your proposal. Examine your own idea carefully. Are you willing to risk failure? Do you trust your idea sufficiently to believe failure is unlikely? If so, proceed. Others rarely object after an idea has proven itself. If they do, you can humbly apologize.

2 ~ *To get what you want, ask for it.*

It is certainly possible that others will recognize what you want and will give it to you before you ask. But it is not likely. To earn what you wish, to get what you want, you must first determine your real desires. Neither inflate nor diminish your needs in making this assessment. Then, ask for what you want.

You will get one of three answers. The answer may be yes. Accept it graciously and do not press for more. The answer may be no. Accept it graciously and begin to think of another way to get your will. Most often, the answer will be noncommittal. Determine what obstacles, if any, present themselves, and prepare an answer to each; set a later date at which to ask again. Never assume that a request, once voiced, remains active; you must ask again until it is answered.

3 ~ *Be excellent, but only in one area.*

Too many undercut their own efforts by attempting excellence in all endeavors. They are, as a result, excellent in nothing. For excellence entails more than correct performance of duties; it means imagination, drive, creativity. Do not delude yourself that you can be truly outstanding in many areas. Let some things slide; no one will be the wiser.

4 ~ *Fluency, not perfection, is most prized.*

The speaker who halts constantly to search for a precise word eventually loses the audience. The fluent speaker, however, keeps our attention and wins our trust. Eloquence is not the opposite of error. To gain eloquence, do not live in fear of making a mistake. An audience better tolerates an occasional misspoken phrase than it does an hour of stammering.

5 ~ *Where there is no shadow, there is only darkness.*

Anyone of substance casts a shadow. It is futile to deny yours. Learn instead to know it as intimately as an old friend. Learn by observing what you are tempted to hate or deride or reject in others. Do you loathe those who flaunt their ambition? Know that you are secretly ambitious. Do you abominate those full of themselves and their ideas? Know that you are secretly centered on your own opinions.

There is no shame in any human possibility. A quality becomes shameful when, banished beyond consciousness, it finds hidden outlets. It is shameful when one who denies her ambition undercuts the work of a favored associate. It is shameful when one who rejects associates as too opinionated harangues others with his own ideas. Do not let this happen: welcome your shadow. Keep it always with you. Know that its presence means that you are standing in light.

6 ~ *You do not have to finish everything today.*

A garden takes time because growth takes time. Each plant grows at an imperceptible pace. Look one day, and the plant is tiny; look the next, it is still tiny. But let it grow undisturbed for a week, and change will become obvious. And by the end of summer, the garden is dense with produce.

So too with ideas and projects. There is rarely a month, a week, even a day for undisturbed work on a single project. The one who waits for such an opening will produce little. It is the one who works steadily at tasks over a long period who becomes accomplished and who accomplishes much. You always have five minutes to spare. Use that time well and consistently, and you will be hailed for what you harvest.

7 ~ *Appear prepared.*

We are not perfect, nor should we appear to be; perfection becomes the basis for others' expectations, so that ordinary performance seems failure. Similarly, we are not always prepared. But we must always appear to be. Prepare carefully whenever you can, but if you are caught unprepared, never reveal it. Never discuss things that could have been done, information that could have been found, ideas that could have been developed. What has not been done, has not been done; do not draw attention to it.

8 ~ *No one knows what you really do.*

It is a mistake to presume that others know what you do. Even your closest associates do not know what your work entails. Those not in direct contact with you certainly do not know.

So do not grow angry when others show ignorance. Know that such ignorance is inevitable, and use it to your advantage. Hide your deficiencies and illuminate your successes. It is for you to decide what others should know of you. It is for you to provide that knowledge. Success is the art of calculated revelation.

9 ~ *Know when you are a unicorn. Know when you are a horse.*

Each of us has two kinds of energies. Before you can use them efficiently, you must distinguish one from the other. The horse energy is strong and sturdy; it allows us to plow through the details of daily work effectively. It is productive, uncomplicated, grounded, thorough. It is also ordinary. The unicorn energy is creative and elusive; it inspires us with new ideas, new visions, new enthusiasms. It is complex, challenging, beautiful. It is extraordinary and infrequent.

Train yourself to recognize unicorn moments and to follow them instantly, for they do not recur.

It is destructive to ignore the unicorn when it appears, for it will slowly visit you less and less frequently. But you must also train yourself to put your horse energy to work. It is no use flogging a horse because it is not a unicorn. Let your horse do the heavy, monotonous work that needs to be done; let your unicorn pass through and illuminate your work with new energies.

10 ~ *Watch your borders.*

You are a sovereign country. However small your territory, do not yield it to invaders. There are those who recognize no borders, who will tramp without cause into your domain. Keep them out with cautious but direct words and with example. There are others for whom any territory, however small, calls forth an urge to mount a campaign of aggression. Learn who these warlords are, and do not trust their slightest action.

It is important that you know your own borders. Learn the exact parameters of your territory. Learn the exact parameters of all adjacent territories. Do not permit vagueness or indifference in this important concern. You need to know exactly where you are at all times.

11 ~ *Protect your boundaries.*

Do no one else's job but your own. Do not answer questions about others' work. Do not be a resource about others' areas of expertise. Do not offer to provide services outside your designated duties. Do not offer advice.

It is easy to unwittingly stray into someone else's territory. Do not do so. You will be greeted as an invader by some, who will then attempt to undermine you in your own territory. Others will appear to welcome you, but later turn on you in anger. Most destructive are those who welcome you and go on welcoming you; they will remain in control of their territory, but you will do their work for them.

12 ~ *Never offer help.*

Animals and children cannot articulate their need for help. And so they whine or cry until someone attends to them. Unless you are dealing with animals or children, ignore all whines and cries. Wait until someone asks you to help. Be certain that you understand the request. Ask for clarification about exactly what you can do. Only then, and willingly and with good heart, should you offer aid.

13 ~ *Never have one without another in its shadow.*

There is never simply one path through mountains. As you travel, always be aware of alternative routes. Who knows when the path on which you have been walking will grow snarled with underbrush or threatened by brigands? Who knows when the one on whom you have depended will be ambushed or abandon you?

Never limit yourself to only one: always have knowledge of others. Know where each turning occurs; remember each branching path. However much you have enjoyed a trail, however much you have found the way easy, however much you wish to continue in a certain direction, there are times when you cannot. You can stand and be lost, or you can turn and be saved. You will have nowhere to turn, however, if you have not attended closely to the route.

14 ~ *Disasters occur, but fires are set.*

When a fire begins, credit accrues to the one who first notices the flames. But sometimes this bystander has more than a passing interest in the event. Sometimes the tinder and oil that began the blaze came, in fact, from the lodgings of the bystander. Secretly, the arsonist creates the inflammatory scene, then seeks to gain by saving the building. Such arson is difficult, if not impossible, to prove. Should you witness such a person's actions, keep him away from your own buildings, and warn your friends to set a fire-watch.

15 ~ *Listen for things that speak themselves.*

Whenever someone speaks, you will hear two messages entwined. One will be the message the speaker wants you to hear. The other will be that which wishes to speak itself. The latter will appear in sentences like a ghost or an invader, at the wrong times, in the wrong places. A person is mentioned who has nothing to do with the subject at hand. Or an irrelevant fact is brought up but not pursued. Watch for these appearances, for these are the secrets on which success is built.

16 ~ *No one is his or her own ancestor.*

Do not argue with the departed. Meet each new person as though there had been no past between your groups. It is useless to argue old problems. It is useless to punish the present officeholder for the abuses of a predecessor. Whatever happened in the past, is past.

17 ~ *Sell to those who are already buying.*

Why should you ignore the one in front of you to draw the attention of one walking past? The passerby does not yet know of you, but the one who is looking at your wares is predisposed to buy. Give your attention to the latter.

Even more important: one who has bought from you once will buy from you again. Go back, go back, go back again to cultivate these friends.

18 ~ *Remember eyes, remember ears, remember hands.*

One person remembers what she sees; another remembers what he hears; others remember what they touch. You must quickly learn this basic fact about each person with whom you deal. Why write to an ear-person, talk to an eye-person, telephone a hand-person? Give what can be taken.

An eye-person remembers what she sees. When she talks, words referring to sight abound. To ask if you understand, she will say, "Do you see?" To demur, she will say, "I don't see what you mean." To affect this person, prepare carefully. Provide pictures, graphs, writings, for each time you meet. Write in response to each meeting, summarizing your discussion. Ask her, "Do you see?" and she will.

An ear-person remembers what he hears. "I hear what you're saying," he will say, or "Did you hear about that?" This person can be affected by stirring words. In dealing with him, practice to the point of eloquence. Use more words, rather than fewer. Use important and impressive words. Organize tightly and explain fully. If you want a hearing, present words that beg to be heard.

The hand-person is frequently in movement. Her very actions express her deep desire to dance through life. Words and images are less important than a sense of flow and action. To affect this person, create a whirlpool around yourself. Take her places; show her how things are done; allow her to touch everything. Whatever she touches, she will remember and concern herself with.

19 ~ *Silence looks like knowledge.*

When you know nothing, speak nothing. Because no one knows what you are thinking, you will appear to be in control of your surroundings. Nod, make notes, appear to ponder. Be very alert. But ask no questions; volunteer no answers. Few can recognize when silence means ignorance, but speech often betrays it.

20 ~ *Tomorrow is your last day.*

Life is not endless, and there are many things more important than merely surviving. Do not indulge in faintheartedness. Do not cling to the past, nor even to the present.

Engage each moment fully. Real success accrues to the one who lives boldly. If you do not live your life as you wish, who will?

21 ~ *Mold your feet to the path.*

Do not expect the path to change because you find it steep. Do not expect a change in scenery because you have grown tired of the view. Do not expect the path to grow wider because you feel constricted. Do not expect it to turn because you are weary of your direction. You cannot change your circumstances; you can only adapt to them.

22 ~ *The demand for instant perfection is the surest path to failure.*

Nothing is born without long gestation. After fecundation are months of growth in darkness. Birth, which seems a beginning, is an end as well. When we focus on the excitement of birth and forget life's hidden development, we fool ourselves into thinking that birth can occur immediately after conception. This has never been so, and it will never be so.

Honor the process of growth in all your endeavors. You may make errors; they can be corrected. You may pursue wrong paths; you can turn back from them. But you can never correct the twisting that occurs when growth is thwarted by a demand for immediate results.

23 ~ *Be firm in everything, rigid in nothing.*

Observe the difference between a living tree and a board made from its wood. The first stands forth in the world, visible to all, standing out against the sky. A fierce wind can uproot it, but its branches sway in the breeze. A board, however, is brittle, rigid. It has no branches to absorb strain. It splinters into dead shards. Learn the difference between firmness and rigidity. Neither yield to everyone nor refuse them all.

24 ~ *Build neither too high nor too low.*

As a bird builds her nest, she must place it with care. Too high, and the spring winds sway the tree so fiercely that the nest is destroyed. Too low, and her nestlings are at risk from predators. Even should she nest each year in the same tree, she must find anew the precise spot, for as the tree grows, it carries away last season's safety and presents new nesting places.

Be like the careful nesting bird. Do not overestimate; you will fail because you cannot support your ideas. But never underestimate; you will be preyed upon by those comfortable at lower ranges. At each stage of your life and your work, take time to determine and consolidate your point of safety.

25 ~ *Prepare for your successor.*

At some time you will be succeeded in every endeavor. Whether job, love, home, remember that someday you will have a new one, and that the one you now occupy will have another occupant. You will leave by one of two routes: you will depart to another job, love, home; or you will die. But you will certainly leave.

There will be an end to this, as to every, experience. Begin now to prepare for the one who comes next. Set things in order. Create systems. Articulate the hidden. A graceful transition means a grateful successor.

26 ~ *A new package means a new product.*

Everyone claims to admire invention, but in fact few do. Many find change unsettling. Should you find yourself responsible to such a frightened person, change appearances regularly, but keep your product the same. Give new names; create new packages; establish new procedures. Save the creation of new things for those who will, in fact, value them.

27 ~ *Dance with, not against, the rhythm.*

There is a pulse, a heartbeat, a tempo to everything. Success lies in finding that rhythm and dancing to it. No one will notice if you are not present during quiet times; everyone will notice your absence during busy periods. Similarly, others will find you difficult if you act whimsically, imposing your mood on the day's plans. Listen for the underlying rhythms around you. Adapt yourself to them first, then improvise your own dance around them.

28 ~ *Learn both to give and to receive praise.*

Criticism is easy, for there are invariably minor faults in any enterprise that you may seize upon to deprecate the whole. Praise is difficult. By praise is not meant wholesale acceptance, but real assessment of someone's or something's best features. Such praise is rare and, because it is rare, is prized. Become the one who ascertains and articulates the best points of each project and each individual. Others are grateful for such attention; you will gain many friends.

When others praise you, accept that praise without demurring. They who praise you do not wish to hear you reject their judgments in favor of your own less favorable ones. Give others the gift of permitting them to praise you without contradiction.

29 ~ *Be sure it is water, not oil, that you throw on the fire.*

Sometimes, in our attempts to douse a fire, we grab whatever is at hand. But what seems a vat of water may instead by filled with oil. Pause and reflect before you do anything in a crisis. You may be only making matters worse. When you do act, be certain that the action is likely to have the intended results.

30 ~ *Ill language breeds ill will.*

Many things go wrong every day. If you remark upon each of them, you will become known as someone full of bad news. Others will come to you only when they wish to hear problems or to share some, and those with good news or solutions will avoid you. Soon enough your world will become poisoned. Others will reflect to you what they believe you wish to know: how difficult life is, how many things go wrong at every turn. You will live in a gloomy world indeed.

Discuss problems, but only in order to seek solutions. Do not malign your work, your co-workers, your superiors, either to friends or to strangers. You may feel you are only scratching an itch, but you may be scarring your reputation.

31 ~ *Observe formalities, but never ironically.*

For those to whom formalities count, they count considerably. Take such matters seriously. There is no cost to you to observe the special days and special customs that give others pleasure and sustenance. Make yourself aware of the occasions and events that matter to those around you. You will gain their loyalty and respect.

Should you believe such customs are foolish or inefficient, it is important that you never reveal this opinion. It is far more insulting to appear to observe a form while commenting upon its triviality than it is to merely ignore it.

32 ~ *Movement causes friction.*

Where there is stasis, there is tranquillity. Where nothing is moving, there is no strain. When all things are at rest, there is no growth or advancement.

When movement occurs, it creates friction. Expect this. The heat engendered through forward movement will cause some sparks to fly. Do not abandon attempts at change because of difficulties you encounter. Lubricate moving parts when needed, but do not halt your motion.

33 ~ *Keep a balance between giving and taking.*

You need not keep a tally sheet on each of your dealings, but you must always know whether you owe more than you are owed, or if the opposite is true. Life is a balance between giving and taking. If you are taking more than you give, you will find that people guard their resources from you, cooperation evaporates, goodwill fails. But if you give more than you take, you will find your stores depleted and your energies exhausted; yet others will return with more demands.

Be aware of two things in each encounter: what is at stake and who is asked to give. Wherever you find a pattern, attempt to change it. If there are people who always ask you for help, go to them and ask the same; if they do not respond quickly and in kind, cease dealing with them. If you frequently ask another for help, know that you must find a way to repay him or her; then do so quickly and fully.

34 ~ *Gossip is a lifeline and a noose.*

No one goes far without information. So learn as much as possible about everything and everyone related to you. Do not listen only to those above you, for often those nearer the ground have better vision. Do not immediately judge information offered you; hear everything, evaluate later. You will hear much that is inexact or untrue; such information will tell you much about its bearer. You will also hear what is true but hidden. Such information offers great advantages.

You must speak as well as listen. If you never gossip, no one will gossip to you; if you gossip constantly, you will never be told secrets. Gossip is precious; reward good informants with jewels of information that they can trade or use. Gossip is costly; never assume what has been told to you has no price, for you become responsible for what you know. And gossip is also risky, for what you have said may be repeated in circumstances that injure you. Never reveal your sources of information, but do not trust that others will similarly keep your confidence. Gossip can tangle and snare your feet; avoid such snarls and those who create them.

35 ~ *Know who your friends are. Know who your allies are. Know the difference.*

It is easier to discover your enemies than it is to learn who your friends are. Enemies will work against you under any circumstances. Friends support you even under duress. Between such categories is a continuum of those who will support you at some times, work against you at others.

It is easy to mistake an ally for a friend. Someone's agreement with you, however often it occurs, is not sufficient for you to assume he or she is a friend. Watch and wait. Let friendship emerge gradually; then let it strengthen before you test it. Until it is as firmly rooted as a tree, do not attempt to take shelter under it.

36 ~ *Watch for the way to open.*

Know what you want, at what you are aiming. Imagine it with as much precision as you can. You cannot find the road unless you know the destination.

Then, when you have ascertained where you wish to be, watch constantly for ways to proceed. It may take time. Circumstances may need to change before you can get there. But unless you have articulated your exact destination, you will miss many opportunities that could lead you in the right direction.

37 ~ *Make common cause with the enemy.*

There is no way to make your enemy your friend. But you can make an ally of an enemy. You need only determine what cause you have in common. Make this a true common cause, not a pretense, for pretending to ally with an enemy only leads to further war. But in any endeavor, there is always a chance for alliance even among those directly opposed in most things. Find and exploit areas of shared concern. You cannot win against your enemy, but forcing him or her to work with you is almost as satisfying.

38 ~ *Consolidate your gains.*

Though it is important to press forward, it is also important to maintain your territory. Do not be always on the move. Stop now and again to survey what you have accomplished and to solidify your gains. These pauses may be short, or they may be long; do not move forward again until you have established order and control over your entire domain. As you do so, new territories will beckon; resist until you are certain all is in order.

39 ~ *Memory lives in the body.*

Your body is not simply a tool for carrying around your head. It is the repository of all your memories. Your body, remembering all that has ever happened to you, can guide you into making swift and accurate judgments. Do not let your body languish while you concentrate solely on your mind, for you will soon lose all drive and force. Do not drive your body by will alone, for that will further destroy your integrity. Work with, not against, the memories and pleasures of your flesh.

40 ~ *It could get worse.*

However difficult things seem now, they could get worse. Do not exaggerate problems. Put them in perspective. Things are almost always better than they seem. Learn optimism; learn to look at what is going right as well as what is going wrong.

41 ~ *Sometimes it is best to let others fight for you.*

Do not assume you must fight every battle for yourself. Sometimes it is most effective, and most efficient, to permit someone else to fight for you. There may be someone whose advantage is served if you win and who will lose nothing if you lose; let that person lead the way into the contest. At other times, an attack is stronger if it comes from an unexpected direction; let your opponent be surprised and unseated. Finally, there may be those with bigger guns than you; certainly let them lead the attack.

42 ~ *Never be a perfect mirror, except to yourself.*

A perfect mirror reflects reality. It reveals imperfections, blemishes, even deformations as clearly as it shows pleasing attributes and qualities. In your own self-reflection, neither underestimate nor overestimate your intelligence, drive, creativity, and charm, or your ambition, greed, and ruthlessness. You need to know yourself thoroughly: you need to recognize all your qualities, whether good or not. It is not helpful to exaggerate your less pleasing qualities, nor is it useful to ignore them. Similarly, it is not to your advantage to derogate your excellent qualities. Be firm and careful in your self-analysis. No one should know you better than you know yourself.

But however much a colleague or superior begs you to provide a perfect reflection, never do so. No one truly wishes to know his or her faults. Nor do people want an unerring—therefore necessarily modest—evaluation of their best qualities. Do not lie to others, either to hide faults or to exaggerate talents, for they will detect such untruths and punish you. Become instead a selective mirror. Give back a reflection of the best each person reveals, magnified only slightly. Praise the passionate for passion, the complacent for calmness, the frightened for caution. There is no need to exaggerate: honor intelligence without calling it genius, enterprise without calling it daring.

43 ~ *If it harms no one, do as you will.*

In any position, there is room to do good and room to do ill. Pursue the first, for what benefits others will bring you renown; avoid the latter, for what harms others may lead to your downfall. But there is also a great neutral ground for action that benefits you but does not help or harm others. It is in this area that the greatest advantage lies.

44 ~ *Speak sooner rather than later.*

Timing is essential in all matters. It is easy to procrastinate, especially when a task is difficult or painful; it is easy to let the proper time pass without action. Speaking truth in order to encourage change is especially difficult. Do not speak immediately; take time to choose your words. But do not avoid the exchange, for problems will mount if you do so. You will speak more calmly, more directly, if you speak of matters in timely fashion.

45 ~ *Call attention to yourself.*

Do not rely on others to call attention to your accomplishments. Especially do not rely upon your superiors, for their role is to encourage a good opinion of themselves alone; they will readily take credit for your good work. Neither rely upon your colleagues, for praising you does not advance them. Instead, find ways to draw the eye gracefully to yourself. Note that gracefulness is of utmost importance: too shameless self-promotion undercuts your efforts. Stress your product, not your involvement in it; emphasize the results, not your effort. You will not gain advancement unless you are recognized. You cannot be recognized if you are invisible.

46 ~ *Do not assume others will act as you would.*

Why should you assume you are the center of the universe? Why should you believe that your actions are the norm? Never express surprise that others act differently than you do, or than you would. Assume, rather, that few will. Do not presume that others are awake when you are awake, sober when you are sober, prepared when you are prepared. Be always aware of the differences between yourself and others. Be always prepared to know more about how they differ from you than you permit them to know about how you differ from them.

47 ~ *There are times to plant, times to harvest, times to prune.*

One who never plants will never harvest, but it is not possible always to initiate and invent. Sometimes you must dedicate your energies to bringing in the results of your initiative. At other times you must thin and prune. Nothing grows well without space and air. Nothing grows well without nourishment. Learn to know when your garden is too crowded, your orchard overgrown. Then cut away to open the way for further growth. Eliminate, eliminate, eliminate.

48 ~ *Give away what you do not need.*

You have some things that you do not need but that others actively covet. Why cling? Give them away. You gain allies with such action. But do not give them away precipitously; a seeker should ask several times before you give an answer. Never give up anything unless you are courted; no one wants anything that seems a discard.

49 ~ *Be the one who says good-bye.*

It is the one who sets the date of departure who has power. Do not let this power escape your grasp. Never let another determine when you will leave. Today—right now—set a date in the future on which you will depart. Do not reveal this date to others, for you will lose power and respect. Change your departure date as you wish, but never lose sight of it. Complacency, conflict, and dissatisfaction set in when a situation seems permanent. Nothing is permanent. Do not delude yourself by thinking otherwise.

50 ~ *Know the difference between fallow and sterile.*

It is sometimes important to withhold action. Sometimes a field must lie fallow to gain strength for later growth. A fallow field is a field at rest. It remains productive, but it is inactive. There is no harm in waiting until a new season for bloom.

But inaction can also mean sterility. A barren field is a place where nothing will grow again. It is not resting; it is dead. Should you find yourself inactive for long periods, examine yourself to see if something in you has died: your imagination, your fantasy, your ambition, your will. Change situations if this occurs, for you will not revive without moving.

51 ~ *Neither undersell nor oversell yourself.*

You must know your own value before you can convince others of it. Search fearlessly to discover all your strengths. But also search fearlessly to discover your weaknesses. Balance each to know yourself; then present this balanced picture to others. Never be too loud in proclaiming your talents, but do not leave them unmentioned either. Be too obvious, and you will alienate others; be too subtle, and you will be ignored and overlooked.

52 ~ *Naming is power.*

Whenever possible, be the one to affix the name to a new product, project, or event, for the one who names has singular power. Do not settle for mere forgettable labels, but search to discover a name that sticks like a burr in the mind. Use few words; use simple words; use words with heart and bone. Speak the name many times, for if it does not rest well on the tongue, it is not a true name.

53 ~ *Goodness, asleep, is the same as evil.*

To do good, you must be active. Sleeping goodness is indistinguishable from evil.

There are two kinds of action goodness can take: positive and negative. Positive goodness means initiating or encouraging what leads to the betterment of our world. Negative goodness means opposing what will damage or destroy our world. Do not wait any longer; take action for the good.

54 ~ *A gift is really an obligation.*

Gifts oblige the receiver. Use gift giving judiciously, for it is a powerful manipulator. If you are the giver, you will seem generous and unselfish, while the one on whom the gift is bestowed will be in your debt. Use this knowledge to your advantage by giving to those whom you wish to control. If you are the receiver, never forget that you are indebted to the giver. Do not let this obligation rest for long. Return something immediately, for unrequited gifts accrue interest at an astonishing rate.

55 ~ *It is easier to kill from roots than from branches.*

Even the most ruthless pruning does not readily destroy something deep-rooted. Deep roots provide amply for replenishment. Even cutting a plant to the ground does nothing if you do not attack the problem at its root. If you wish to completely eradicate something, go to its deepest level and remove it there.

56 ~ *Never argue with a critic.*

When someone criticizes you, listen carefully. Agree where possible; otherwise do not speak. It is of no use to argue or to defend yourself. The critic is not interested in learning why something occurred; the critic is only interested in expressing disdain, dismay, or disappointment. Should you wish to respond, do so afterward. Respond calmly and without defensiveness, giving no cause for further comment or complaint.

57 ~ *In small matters, always do as you promise.*

Nothing undercuts success so quickly as a reputation for breaking your word. Yet few recall big promises, while everyone remembers small ones. Promise another that you will deliver a bushel of gold in a year, and he or she will promptly forget. But promise to deliver a single piece of paper, and you will be watched until it is done. Avoid promising small favors unless you are certain you can provide them.

58 ~ *Out is the same as up.*

There are times when it is impossible to climb further. The way may be blocked by others, or there may be no footholds, or you may have reached the top of a rise too small for your ambition. Do not hesitate, in such circumstances, to climb elsewhere. There is little likelihood that mountains will grow smaller, or that blockages will be removed, or that footholds can be carved. Other climbs await you. Go.

59 ~ *Find the good in the powerful.*

Everyone has good qualities, and it is imperative that you find them in your superiors. It is far easier to locate a powerful person's flaws than to find his or her sterling qualities. Play to a powerful person's best side, and you will become a trusted confidant.

60 ~ *Say no pleasantly; say yes fiercely.*

Temper your messages. Too enthusiastic a yes suggests that you are overeager, immature, unconfident. Too stern a no suggests that you are impolitic, malicious, niggardly. Be cool and distant when you offer approval; be warm and supportive when you must criticize. You will thus avoid causing those whom you approve to ask for more or those you deny to become vengeful.

61 ~ *Provide closure for yourself.*

In raising a child, you do not look for an ending, for only death ends a parent's responsibilities. Many tasks are like this. Yet it is natural to yearn for a sense of completion in life and in work. Therefore invent and maintain moments of closure. Just as a child's birthday party represents a completed year of growth, so rituals and ceremonies can be used to create endings where none naturally exist.

Break complex projects into many smaller projects, and celebrate the conclusion of each. Break a year into seasons, and celebration the successes of each. Establish occasions that are unique to your position, and reward yourself when milestones are reached. If you do this, you will be both happier and more productive.

62 ~ *It takes time to manage time.*

You must spend time managing your schedule to greater benefit. Failure to manage time efficiently begins when you forget this simple rule. Make time in your schedule to plan both long-range and short-range goals. Organize each into manageable units of completion. Create a schedule, and hold fiercely to it.

Be certain to include some personal goals in your planning. Nothing so quickly undermines a life as too single-minded a devotion to duty. Know what you wish to attain on a personal level, and plan how to attain it.

63 ~ *Better too little than too much.*

When offered a chance to speak, use as few words as possible. Stop while your auditors are still rapt in your words, and you will give the impression of having more and valuable thoughts. Continue after they have ceased to be interested, and even your best thoughts will be forgotten.

In writing, too, brevity is a virtue. Concentrate your information in a single paragraph, and you will gain your objective. Extend it through several pages, and you will dilute your effectiveness.

64 ~ *Give them what they pay for.*

You may be tempted to cut corners on quality in order to save time. Do so at your peril. Shoddy work is rarely forgiven. A recipient who instantly forgets good work will remember inadequate work for years. Reputation is of paramount importance. Do not risk yours because of haste or impatience.

65 ~ *Never complain of success.*

Success breeds envy. Should you attain a position of prominence, be aware that others resent you more than they admire you. Therefore avoid complaining of factors that inhibit you from succeeding even more notably. Certainly such factors exist; they may even cause you great pain. But why look ungracious and ungrateful by describing them?

66 ~ *Know exactly how vulnerable you are.*

It is easy to underestimate or overestimate the instability of your position. Should you do the former, you may act rashly, thinking yourself more solidly settled than you are. This could be your downfall. Should you do the latter, you may be too cautious and unimaginative. This too could be your downfall, for inaction when action is needed undermines your reputation.

You must continually survey your position to know how secure, or insecure, it is. Know who supports you and why; act to assure their continued support. Know your talents and strengths; work to let others know of them. Know too your weaknesses; work to correct or disguise them. No one should know more about you than you yourself.

67 ~ *Not to act is still to act.*

Do not convince yourself that inaction is different from action. Sometimes, indeed, it is better not to act, not to speak, not to press an issue, not to pursue a program. In such cases, you must actively decide not to act. Putting off a decision is itself a decision. Avoiding action is itself an action. Make such choices only when it serves your aims.

68 ~ *A strong end is more important than a strong beginning.*

The one who crosses the finish line first is always the one who wins. The race does not necessarily go to the one who starts fastest, whose early stride is longest, who is ahead at the half. You will be evaluated primarily on how you conclude a program or a project. Start strongly if you can; continue strongly if you can. But remember, always end strongly.

69 ~ *Go ahead, ask for more.*

Because something has already been negotiated does not mean that negotiations cannot be reopened. You will doubtless be turned away at first, for one to whom an arrangement is advantageous will be slow to change it. But sometimes factors have changed that make renegotiating necessary. Ask, and you may be denied. If you never ask, however, you will certainly never receive.

70 ~ *Do not settle for what you never wanted.*

Do not convince yourself that what you want is merely what you are offered. Assess your desires and your needs; articulate them to yourself. Know them firmly and surely. When something else is offered, recognize its difference, and its distance, from your goals. Accept it temporarily if you need to, but move on to something closer to your goal as soon as possible. In this, your one life, you must not settle for less than the best.

71 ~ *Only rescue those who will not drown you.*

There are times when you cannot rescue another. When the water is too deep, when your stroke is not strong enough, when the other is flailing too dangerously, you must resist the temptation to play lifeguard. Assess yourself, your abilities, your strength. Assess the water and the weather. If you can, offer aid, even when there is some risk. But if there is no hope of saving the one who is sinking, do not create another bloated corpse. Swim away. Swim away.

72 ~ *Let coyote out to play.*

Do not tie the hands of the fool. Do not gag the fool's mouth. What seems like nonsense is often the best sense. What seems like play is often the highest form of creative work. Let the coyote out of its cage. Go ahead, romp and tease. Run and leap. There must be joy in every endeavor. The trickster, the fool, the coyote, returns joy to where there has been only strained effort.

73 ~ *To increase the harvest, nurture the seedling.*

Ideas and projects, when small, are delicate. Now, when things are burgeoning, offer only water and sun. Let growth take its natural course for a while. What is not hardy will soon wither. What is hardy but not yet perfect needs time to strengthen sufficiently to survive. There is time later to prune and transplant. Save your criticism and analysis; this is the wrong time for them.

74 ~ *Smile when you attack.*

Attack only when you need to; it depletes your resources and creates enemies. When you must attack, choose the time and place carefully so that all things work to your advantage. When you are on the attack, you are most vulnerable yourself. Do not leave your own citadel unguarded in order to launch out against another. In the stress of battle you may be yourself destroyed.

Choose to attack when you know you have the strength for it, rather than gauging only the weakness of your enemy. Choose to attack when you know you are willing to lose what you have in order to gain greatly, or when you care more for what is at stake than you care for your safety. Commit yourself wholeheartedly to the battle. And smile as you thrust home.

75 ~ *Absorb what is useful. Ignore what is not useful.*

You do not need to reject that which serves no purpose. It is enough to avoid or to evade that which does not advance you. Negation uses energy better applied elsewhere. Shun the temptation to eradicate what simply fails to serve you at this moment. Instead, focus on locating what nourishes you, what gives you strength and power. Absorb these into your essence.

76 ~ *Never imagine that your leader is your friend.*

It is the duty of a leader to lead. Some leaders are charming, some stern; some leaders are friendly, some aloof. But no matter what your leader's personality, remember that his or her duty does not include offering friendship to you. Do not confide in or commiserate with your leader. You will only lose what you have and will gain nothing.

77 ~ *First fill the purse, then ask for what you need.*

If you have a full purse, others will listen. If you have an empty purse, they will not. You may, in fact, be ignored or targeted by others. There is no guarantee that monetary success will bring what else you want and need. But monetary failure certainly will not. Fill the purse first. You will then have the basis on which to ask for resources, people, even freedom.

78 ~ *Speed is vital. Haste is not.*

An immediate response need not be a hasty one. Know the difference between working fast and working too fast. The first is prized; the second creates more problems than it solves. There are times when a quick response is demanded but is in fact unnecessary; to submit to such a demand merely weakens you. But at other times an immediate reply will strengthen your position. At such times, focus utterly on the task at hand, and allow no interruptions until you have completed it. Make a brief but exact reply. Do not let time pass before your response is heard and felt.

79 ~ *Keep the self to the self.*

The self is infinitely complex and complicated. It is not a unity that must present itself in all facets at once and in all situations at once. Turn the most appropriate face toward each person. If need be and occasion arises, turn another face, and then yet another. No one ever needs to see the entirety of you. Perhaps no one can.

80 ~ *Begin negative, end positive.*

We usually first tell others what is generally good about their work, then provide critical specifics about what is wrong. The listener then obviates the praise, remembering only the criticism that followed it, or the listener never hears the praise at all, being acutely aware that criticism will follow. Reverse the order: first give general critical comments, then follow with specific praise. We remember what we hear last, so you will be remembered as praising rather than attacking. You will both correct deficiencies and boost morale.

81 ~ *Chaos is the most exquisite order.*

In the heart of order lies chaos, and in the heart of chaos, order. Great sweeping arcs of pattern can be discerned even in what appears to be random. And it is within that chaos that we find the most creative ideas. Look deeply into the owl face of chaos, for there wisdom hides.

82 ~ *You must change your life.*

Change is constant. You can either manage it or be destroyed by it. If you resist or ignore change, it will crush you. If, however, you seek ways to change your own life, you can thrive in circumstances that would ruin the less flexible. Constant small changes relieve the pressure, which builds up like pressure in a fault across the earth's crust. Relieve that pressure, and you will avoid earthquakes.

83 ~ *Review everything, even what you think is settled.*

Never imagine that a problem, once settled, remains settled. Even the most silent volcano is slowly building up pressure under its lava dome, to erupt long after you would have believed it dead. Do not forget to check up on what seems to run smoothly. It is there where problems are growing.

84 ~ *You never know who is listening.*

It is common to assume that you can speak freely when, in fact, you should not. It is also common to imagine that you know everything important about someone you are addressing. Beware of such misapprehensions. The clerk in a cafe may be the daughter of your enemy. The empty hallway hides a half-open door. The telephone line misconnects to permit eavesdropping. Be aware of all you say; be ready to stand behind it. It is foolishness to lose pride or position for a jest or a half-meant rudeness.

85 ~ *A liar needs a good memory.*

Lies are a necessary part of life. They serve to keep distance between those who are not connected or are at odds. Be aware that not everyone has the right to know everything that you do or that you know. But lies should be used only as a last resort, when imagination or inspiration fail. It is far better to refuse to answer or to divert a question than it is to lie. For your listener will remember what you say and will notice any later divergence. You cannot be held accountable for limited or withheld information; you can be held accountable for misinformation.

86 ~ *No explanation ever suffices to deflect criticism.*

When someone has determined that you have done wrong, no explanation—no matter how reasonable—will convince that person otherwise. Do not waste your breath on defending yourself. Accept the criticism with as few words as possible. Any words will be wasted, for guilt exists in the eye of the accuser rather than in the actions of the accused.

87 ~ *Follow your leader.*

When your leader departs, you should depart. Learning to follow a new leader is more difficult than moving your camp to the new battlefield. If you have been successful in one place under a leader, you will be successful elsewhere under that leader. If you have been unsuccessful, the new leader will blame you, not the departed leader, for the poor record. Prepare to leave with or shortly after your leader.

If you must remain, neither condemn nor praise your earlier leader. Condemnation will make you appear disloyal, fickle. Enthusiastic praise will make your new leader feel inadequate and competitive. Be mildly approving of your previous leader at all times, for thus you appear a dedicated follower, worthy of the confidence of your new superior.

88 ~ *Be the one who acts first.*

The one who makes the first move is seen as assertive and organized; the one who responds, as reactive and disorganized. It is very simple to be thought the first, rather than the second. For any project, initiate a call, a letter, a meeting, a committee; do this at regular intervals, whether weekly or monthly. This is especially effective in dealing with those who do not seem to respect you. If you respond to them only when they contact you, you will quickly find that they believe you to be disorganized at best, lazy at worst. But if they hear from you regularly—even if you contact them only on minor matters—they will soon believe that you are a diligent worker who has their best interests at heart.

89 ~ *You are not in Kansas anymore.*

Look around yourself constantly to evaluate your current position. Even without moving, you may find you are in a new situation, one that calls for new skills and new ideas. The most difficult transition to manage is that in which you stand still but the world moves furiously around you. Fight the tendency to hold onto your vision of the past. Adjust yourself constantly to the realities of your life.

90 ~ *Money is made in the gray areas.*

If something is known to be profitable, there will be many players in that field. If something is known to be not profitable, there will be no players. The greatest profits lie in areas that are still developing, new, or ripe for rebuilding. Profiting in such areas requires careful study and shrewd intuition. Define yourself a portion of the gray-area market, develop it carefully, and move on when the fields have been harvested.

91 ~ *Five minutes of preparation is worth hours of reparation.*

Always take time to prepare for upcoming events and meetings. It is far more effective to spend time beforehand than to attempt to repair damage done by lack of preparation. Such preparation also allows you to take initiative and turn the tide of events in your selected direction.

92 ~ *Never come between a mother bear and her cubs.*

A good leader will never turn upon his or her followers. It is ineffective to attempt to drive a wedge between them. Should you object to the actions of a subordinate, bring this to the leader's attention in the presence of the offending party. But do not attempt to get the leader to take your side at that point. If you are dealing with excellence, you will find only support and understanding for the subordinate in the presence of others. Any discipline will take place out of your sight and earshot.

Similarly, you should be a strong, supportive leader to your own subordinates. Do not undercut them—even jokingly—in the presence of others. You need not defend them when conduct has been indefensible, but do not attack them either. All discipline should be between leader and follower, with no witnesses.

93 ~ *The world will not stop because you wish it.*

Change is constant in this universe. At all times, something is changing. There are times when you wish the world would stop in its ceaseless flux, give you a chance to catch up and relax. But nothing will cause the world to stop. You must learn to create for yourself the spaces that permit you to reach closure on projects, to develop new ones, to create and to destroy. If you wait passively for the world to provide you with a calm haven, you will wait forever.

94 ~ *Be alert for those who cannot share.*

For some, ownership is everything. There are those for whom sharing is impossible. Notice how such a one transforms every idea, every project, every event, into a possession. Notice how such a one removes all vestige of your involvement. There is no working with a person like that. Know that you will either give up much, or be constantly at war, or—most effective of all—provide many illusions of control while keeping control to yourself. Let the selfish have much, so long as it is unnecessary to you; appear as though you regret what you have lost. Keep what is necessary, and never gloat or draw attention to it.

95 ~ *Never let betrayal take you by surprise.*

Do not expect people to treat you well because that is what you deserve. Betrayal is as frequent as sunrise. Always know who in your terrain is prone to betrayal, and expect it of them. For some people, betrayal is a habit they cannot break; eventually they will betray you, no matter how helpful you have been, or how diligent or how enthusiastic or how intelligent. Traitors are traitors.

Harder to discover are those who resort to this behavior only occasionally. Sometimes they do not intend to betray you; sometimes they are forced by circumstance; sometimes they are utterly unwitting, but destructive nonetheless. Be alert to hints of betrayal; contradictions and ambiguities often disguise an intent to victimize you. Watch especially for discrepancies between action and speech, for rarely can a traitor remain convincing in both realms at once.

96 ~ *Do not always do what is expected.*

Learn to keep your opponents on guard by changing your strategies frequently. Do not become predictable, as this will be used against you. Know your own most common strategies more deeply than your opponents do, so that you can change quickly when the situation demands. Are you usually vocal? Sometimes be silent. Are you usually cooperative? Sometimes be demanding. Are you usually reliable? Sometimes be late. Use the power of surprise to gain advantage.

97 ~ *Do it now. Deal with it immediately.*

Do not wait until minor annoyances become major problems. Deal with each circumstance as it occurs. What is put off becomes abhorrent: we loathe what we have so far failed to complete. Most battles begin because something has been unsaid, unexamined, for too long. Each day is a new opportunity. Deal with the matters of that day before the sun sets.

98 ~ *Be careful whom you advise.*

You do not need to tell everything you know. Advice is precious. Give it forth judiciously. Advice unsought is often resented; advice unsought is rarely valued. Make it a rule never to advise anyone whom you casually meet and to rarely advise those with whom you are close. When you choose to offer information, opinion, or advice, draw attention to the fact that you are doing so.

When suitable, ask for a return for your assistance, even if it is only gratitude.

99 ~ *Deliver the blow swiftly.*

It is hard to hurt others. So, trying to avoid hurting our followers and colleagues, we hurt them more. We neglect or put off announcing bad news, thus generating rumor and fear. We shy away from revealing damning information, thus limiting another's response. We forget to file important documents, thus creating additional disorder and difficulty.

Then, when we finally deliver the blow, we are angry at ourselves for our procrastination and hit harder than necessary. This is selfish and cruel. When you must strike, do so quickly and cleanly. It does not advance you, or save your victim, to evade or avoid.

100 ~ *The later it grows, the more odious grows the task.*

A task avoided becomes loathsome. When a task is newly assigned or imagined, you find it attractive and interesting. Begin work on it immediately, while you have fresh vision and a sense of possibility. If possible, continue until completion, for the interruption of tasks creates a burden that is soon transferred onto the task itself. This in turn leads to further avoidance, until performance seems impossible. Though you may eventually flog yourself into finishing the task, you will waste much effort conquering your resistance. Whenever possible, organize your work so that tasks are assigned, begun, and accomplished without interruption.

101 ~ *Do not stand out in the wind, even to find out which way it blows.*

Winds of change blow constantly, sometimes from this direction, sometimes from that. It is more important to recognize that wind is a constant factor than it is to know exactly which direction it blows today. Watch the weather vane to determine its direction and, if necessary, make adjustments. But do not court disaster by standing out in the wind. Change will affect you in any case. Do not endanger yourself by recklessly standing in its way.

102 ~ *If it can be mended, mend it. If it cannot, destroy it.*

There is an art to knowing what can be fixed and what is beyond repair. Much effort is wasted on attempting to repair the ruined or to resuscitate the drowned. But there is waste, too, in destroying what can be salvaged. You need to do more than simply weigh cost in determining which approach to take. Your calculations must include a prophetic view of future developments. You must imagine, in detail, the future of the object, the relationship, the project. And then you must act wholeheartedly. Do not partially sustain what is unsustainable. Do not partially smother what gasps for life. Take action quickly and fully.

103 ~ *Guard your weakness well.*

Never ask for sympathy; it will rarely be forthcoming. Rather, others may abandon or persecute you if they perceive that you are weak. Keep your weaknesses secret. Let others work to discover them. Why offer others the knowledge that allows them to benefit at your expense?

104 ~ *If you put something off long enough, you will be interrupted.*

Admit it, there is something you are resisting doing. It is no use pretending that the task is not there awaiting you. It is there, and it will remain there until you put your hand to it. Set time aside and perform the task right through to completion. Or divide the task into smaller parts and complete one. Do not sit there resisting, for if you resist long enough, another task will demand your attention, and the primary task will still remain uncompleted. Just act.

105 ~ *Time can be a barrier or a path.*

You can use time to set up barriers between yourself and others. The one who is unavailable, who cancels appointments, who changes meetings—that is the one with power. The one who rearranges schedules, who waits for a meeting that never starts, who is endlessly available—that is the one without power. Do not use time barriers simply to avoid conflict or frustration; use them constructively, to heighten your image. Or use time to build paths: let those you wish to cultivate know you are available to them.

106 ~ *There is no guarantee that sisters will be friends.*

There is never any reason to assume friendliness, even when circumstances or relationships seem to warrant it. Assistance is always a gift, never an obligation. Never presume that it will be offered, even where it has been offered previously. Neither presume that one who has never offered help will never do so. Deal with each person afresh each time you meet.

107 ~ *Speak only when you have considered all the consequences.*

Honesty is not always the best policy. It is often tempting to speak your mind, to clear the air, to put your cards on the table. Think carefully before you do so. Think through all possible consequences, and weigh whether the pleasure of expressing yourself is worth the risk. For there is risk each time you speak.

You cannot speak without paying. Ask yourself before speaking, Am I willing to pay for this pleasure? If not, remain silent. If so, speak cleanly and eloquently, without holding back. Then begin to establish your defensive strategy immediately afterward, for you will need it.

108 ~ *Gratitude meets obligations.*

When people do things for you, you must repay them. Whether they acknowledge it or not, they will be keeping score. If you do not offer repayment, they will begin to withhold from you. You may lose allies in this fashion. If you do not have something to offer immediately, however small, offer your gratitude in a gesture as well as in words. The gesture will be remembered, and the obligation met.

109 ~ *It is rarely effective to show anger.*

Meet anger with anger, and you will find yourself embroiled in trouble. While another rages at you, find stillness within yourself and retreat to it, for this is not a time when you will be heard. Meet injustice with anger, and you will raise defenses that can, in turn, grow into greater injustice and more aggression. Anger, even righteous anger, is rarely effective. Bite your tongue, and plan for an expression of your anger that can be heard and will be effective.

110 ~ *You need not answer every request.*

Power rests in the denial, as well as the fulfillment, of requests. Do not feel you need to approve each and every request. Do not fall into the trap of denying them all, either, for you will soon gain a reputation for being difficult, even lazy. But it does you no good to answer every demand. Demands that come at unusual times, that require unusual resources, that are outside your expertise—these should be denied. But you have the power as well to decline to fulfill requests that you are qualified and able to perform, if there is no payback to you. If you are not saying no to one-quarter of the requests that come your way, you are doing more than you need to.

111 ~ *Go ahead, move the furniture.*

Sometimes you need to make a visible, tangible movement that shows that you have taken charge. Sometimes something as simple as rearranging the furniture will do. There are other ways: change your schedule, wear different clothing, cut your hair. Human beings are not only minds; we are bodies. Our bodies respond to changes in our surroundings. Your control over the details of your surroundings is part of your command of your life.

112 ~ *Improve the best, work on the next best, eliminate the worst.*

Do not expend energy on what is already unsuccessful while slighting what works. Do the reverse: support and expand the best you have to offer; locate and retire the worst. Success breeds success. When something is growing, feed it, so that it will grow more. Why withhold water from a thriving plant? What is already weak requires much effort to make it strong. What is already strong requires little to make it outstanding.

113 ~ *A blue sky now does not guarantee good weather tomorrow.*

Never let calm weather make you overconfident. When others are helpful, ask yourself what they have to gain by helpfulness. When others are kind, ask yourself what kindness gains them. Do not let yourself become lulled into believing that no storm can touch you. Better to prepare for stormy weather than to be becalmed and later betrayed.

114 ~ *Death never gives a year's warning.*

No matter how hard you work, no matter how foresightful you attempt to be, there are some things that surprise you. It is futile to rail against the inevitable. Your only strategy should be to know that you cannot control everything. Then work fully and responsibly in the present, and accept surprises when they come.

115 ~ *Do not speak about what is not yet accomplished.*

It is tempting to talk about feats yet to be achieved, deals yet to be closed, projects yet to be approved. Avoid this. Nothing dissipates energy as quickly as talk. You need to reserve your energy to perform. Talk dissolves your will to perform. It satisfies the same urge to produce, to create, as production and creation themselves. Although it is difficult to preserve silence in the face of excitement, it is also the best strategy.

116 ~ *It does not help to put off the inevitable.*

Do it now, that task you dread. It does no good to put off what you must eventually do. It only builds annoyance on the part of the person to whom you must respond and annoyance as well on your part as you consider the task. Take yourself in hand and act. You will rest easier.

117 ~ *Vengeance on a fox is impossible.*

Vengeance has limited use. Sometimes—rarely—it is justified by egregiously bad behavior. Mostly, it flatters the avenger with a sense of power. And in some cases it creates even more damage. Some opponents will enter guerrilla warfare with anyone who attempts to punish them. Weigh your cause carefully before you attempt to wreak vengeance, however well merited it might seem.

118 ~ *Never attempt to reason with the irrational.*

It is a waste of time to try logical arguments against irrationality. Emotion has its own logic, one that can readily ensnare you. You are surrounded by the irrational. Meet it on its own terms. Center yourself in your heart, and deal from there: emotion answering emotion. Remember, too, that emotion responds to command. Express yourself commandingly. Avoid the swamp of intent, the bog of meaning: do not involve yourself in discussions of what you meant by what you said. Speak carefully, sharply, clearly. That is enough.

119 ~ *Tomorrow will be better.*

Everything passes. Even the deepest emotion passes. The bliss of love fades. The most bitter tears cease to flow. Whatever is happening now, know that something different will happen tomorrow. If things are bad, realize that they will get better. If things seem calm, realize that they could easily become stormy. Always be aware of change. Work with it to your advantage.

120 ~ *It never hurts to look again.*

Do not give up if you do not find what you need immediately. It is there, but you must discover it. What you need—advice, money, love—will make its presence known if you search long and trustingly enough. Do not become discouraged by apparent failures. You will succeed. Believe that.

121 ~ *It cannot hurt to hope.*

Why believe that negative predictions are truth but optimistic ones fantasy? There is as much chance that the best will come of any situation than that the worst will happen. So go ahead and hope. Sometimes hope in itself will change an outcome for the better. Similarly, despair can create bad conditions or worsen them. Nothing is lost by looking on the bright side.

122 ~ *Those who have white dogs should not wear black clothes.*

Look honestly at yourself and then admit what is unchangeable. Work with what you have rather than denying what is obvious to all. Struggling against yourself only draws attention to your defects. Learn to hide them by working with them. Wear white clothes if you have white dogs; stray hairs will not be noticed. Find ways to work with, rather than against, yourself.

123 ~ *Drought follows deluge follows drought.*

Everything progresses in cycles. A period of creativity, when your ideas seem to flow readily, will always be followed by a time when you seem to have no ideas at all; that, in turn, will flow into another period of inspiration. Similarly, periods when you seem to be productive and organized will alternate with chaotic periods. Do not bemoan the season. Use inspiration when it appears; in the fallow periods, prepare yourself for later expansion. During productive periods, complete what you can; use chaotic periods to begin new work. Season follows season. Do not sow in winter, nor lie fallow in summer.

124 ~ *If you do not ask for it, the answer is always no.*

Cowardice and timidity bring you to the same place: nowhere. If you wish to move ahead, you must take steps. These steps will entail risk, for you cannot advance without risk. But you risk relatively little by making a request. And you are unlikely to gain your desire through silence and passivity. You gain neither power nor influence by standing still and hoping you will be noticed.

125 ~ *Guard well your purse.*

In any negotiation, remember that your interests are not the same as the other party's. Give way on many things, but do not give way on money until all other areas of compromise have been exhausted. It is in the interest of your opponent to gather resources; it is in your interest to do the same. Give up time, give up titles, give up the trappings of power. But keep your pocket guarded well.

126 ~ *Lions should never stoop to fight with rabbits.*

If you wish to command, resist the impulse to lessen yourself through contention and conflict. Rarely is it worthwhile to attack those above you; you are more likely to be bloodied than to bloody them. But do not waste yourself on conflict with those beneath you. Even should you win, victory will be short-lived, for another conflict will immediately arise; those who wish to bring you down will learn that you respond to their taunting. You will soon be caught in an endless cycle of conflict, response, more conflict.

Withdraw from the arena. Refuse to fight. Conflict will slowly lessen.

127 ~ *Speak first, and you lose.*

Judicious silence is the first rule of negotiation. Let others speak first. They will reveal their flaws as well as their needs. You can then play upon their flaws, meet or deny their needs. Speaking last puts you in the position of power. Withhold, withhold.

128 ~ *It is not about personality; it is about power.*

What seems to be a personal conflict between people is, invariably, not so: it is a struggle for power. The search for power disguises itself in many ways. One of the most common is the inability to work smoothly with one who holds, or could hold, power. When there is something to be gained for each, even very difficult people can work together smoothly. When there is power at stake, even compatible people can argue. Watch carefully wherever personality seems to be an issue. A power struggle is brewing there.

129 ~ *You are doing exactly what you want.*

Do not tell yourself that you would rather be doing something else. If you were, you would not be doing what you are doing. Some part of you wants to stay where you are. That part of you has immobilized the part that wishes to move. What do you gain from remaining where you are? What need do you satisfy by standing still?

130 ~ *What you give to others, you yourself desire.*

Examine what you offer to others. Are you friendly and cooperative? That is because you wish others to offer you help. Are you challenging, demanding? You wish others to set standards for you. You give to others what you hope to get yourself. Try offering the friendliness, the challenge, to yourself first. If you cannot provide your own needs, you cannot really provide others' needs either.

131 ~ *Admitting mistakes does not mean accepting blame.*

It is important to admit mistakes, for we all make mistakes. This does not mean, however, that you should accept blame from others—or from yourself. Blaming cannot erase the past and can only hurt you. Refuse to accept blame. You have tried and failed, but that is better than not trying. If you do nothing, you will certainly avoid mistakes. That you have sometimes failed means you are active, moving forward. Do not be defensive about your mistakes. Acknowledge them, then move on.

132 ~ *Once is an accident. Twice is coincidence. Three times means you have an enemy.*

Do not believe anyone who tells you that a repeated difficulty is not intentional. Nothing happens more than twice without intent. Always be aware of the patterns around you. Examine them for cause and for intent. Defend yourself when necessary. And remember that often awareness itself is the best defense.

133 ~ *When attacked, defend by silence.*

It is rarely effective to defend yourself with words against an attack upon your work or upon your character. Defense invariably sounds defensive. Silence speaks volumes. Your attacker, faced with silence, will reiterate, reinforce, exaggerate the attack. Soon it will become clear that the cannon is of too great a caliber for the offense, and the attacker's destructive motives will become plain. Support for your opponent will dissipate, and you will have won.

134 ~ *Use what weapons are to hand.*

When attacked, do not stop and forge a new weapon perfectly suited for response. Use what is nearby. Use your time to select wisely from among what is already prepared. Do not bemoan your lack of the perfect weapon. As a corollary to this, you should always be preparing weapons. Even when no attack is visible, one is brewing. Prepare before an attack, and your weapons will come nearer to perfection.

135 ~ *Ignore words, look to deeds.*

Examine what you expect from each person, then observe that person's behavior. You may trust some people wrongly, expecting them to assist you when they have never done so previously. Or you may suspect someone wrongly, assuming ill intent when he or she presents no such difficulties. Look to deeds, not words, to determine whom to trust, whom to avoid, whom to assist, whom to refrain from assisting.

136 ~ *Grasp by the handle, not the blade.*

There are two approaches to any problem. One makes things easier, one more difficult. One makes the problem into a tool to make change in your life; one hurts you, perhaps injures you deeply. Examine the problem and determine which way to grasp hold of it to make it work for you. Then grasp, and make change.

137 ~ *You must always know where home is.*

It is harder to fight when you are away from home; it is harder to win when you are on another's court. You must learn to find your home within, learn to touch down into your heart's home no matter how far you seem to have traveled. Be like the turtle: with a rock-shell, protect your inner home, your heart of hearts. It is from that beating strength within that you prevail.

138 ~ *Sit on the shady porch in hot weather; stoke the fire when it snows.*

Adapt yourself to the climate. The climate cannot adapt itself to you, nor can you force it to change. Those who survive and who succeed are those who are willing to change. Do not be rigid or unbending. Study the customs of your comrades. Align yourself with them wherever possible. Wearing heavy clothing in the sun, standing with bare arms in the driving snow—how can these help you advance?

139 ~ *Do not worry. Simply face the truth.*

Worry is a useless expenditure of energy. The mind creates endless alternative paths, all of them ending in disaster or futility. Why waste your time? Learn the truth and live with it; this will put the worry from your mind. If you are doing all you can to learn the truth, put the worry from your mind. If you wish to refuse to face reality, make that choice—then put the worry from your mind.

140 ~ *When the right door opens, walk through it.*

You are in a huge hall with many doors opening out from it. At any moment, one or two doors will be open. One may be open wide, another only a crack. Do not judge an opening by wideness alone: the most open door may lead to nothing. But do not waste your time pounding on closed doors. Demanding an opening will not make it occur. Watchfulness is what you need—watchfulness, and a keen sense of where each opening leads.

141 ~ *There are sweet harvests as well as bitter ones.*

What we plant grows and finally must be harvested. Look around you, and notice what is ready to be picked. Pick it, then move on. What you do not pick will rot and become dangerous. Even if the seed was not exactly what you desired, what you have grown is your fruit; own it. If you always find the harvest bitter, think more carefully each time you plant, and remember, you are always planting, planting every moment.

142 ~ *A wish is not a goal.*

You say you want something? Then make it your goal. Do not just wish for it. Wishing does nothing. A wish is swaddled in the gauze of dream. It is intangible, out of reach. A goal is hard as diamond. It can be touched. Because it can be touched, it can be attained. Once you have created a goal, you will know what steps you must take to attain it. But if a wish, a dream, resists becoming concrete, honor that: it needs to remain yet in the soft comfort of unchallenged desire.

143 ~ *Weather is not climate.*

Even the longest heat wave has finally an ending. There is no snow that does not someday melt. The one constant about weather is that it changes. Climate, however, in unchangeable: if you want icebergs, do not go to the desert; if you want cactus, do not lodge on a glacier. Distinguish what is climate, what is weather. If you cannot stand the climate, move; if you do not like the weather, just wait.

144 ~ *Promises, not problems.*

Each day is an account book with debts and assets. It is always tempting to look at your debts and be overwhelmed. But many rich people carry great debt; many memorable days begin with problems. Look to your assets. Emphasize them rather than taking them for granted. Build upon them. No matter to whom you speak, speak of promises rather than problems.

145 ~ *It is always easier to continue than to start.*

It is always hard to start a rock rolling down a hill. But once it is rolling, it moves more and more quickly, until something finally stops it. Do not yourself provide stopping places for your dreams; do not impede their forward progression. Keep rolling, even if that means moving only a small way each day.

146 ~ *A cracked egg can be spoiled, or it can be hatching.*

Sometimes opportunity appears as difficulty. When we see a thin line cracking across an egg's shell, we may assume the egg is spoiled and throw it away. But perhaps that crack indicates the emergence of new life. Wait; let the difficulty make itself plainer, or let the opportunity reveal itself. No harm will come of a moment's patience.

147 ~ *First things first.*

Do what is important immediately. Do not put it off. You do not need to warm up to importance; you do not need to be in the mood. The secret of success is accomplishing what is important, not completing many unimportant things. Imagine that you can accomplish only one thing today. What would that be? Do that. Do it right now.

148 ~ *Accidents never happen when you expect them.*

Prepare constantly for difficulty. At any time, plans may go awry. If you work as though accidents cannot happen, they will utterly disrupt your plans. Allow slack and "give" in every situation; provide room for the inevitable difficulties. Then, when an accident happens, you can better handle it than if you had expected perfection.

149 ~ *What would happen if you just walked away?*

Put things in perspective: what would really happen if you just walked away? What would you lose if you left behind what is hurting you? You need not stay where you are; there are other places you could occupy, possibly more happily than where you are now. What keeps you where you are? If there is nothing, walk away. If there is something, you will know why you stay.

150 ~ *You must weed in every season.*

No matter how carefully you have planted, weeds can choke the garden. One of your tasks is constant weeding, to assure that your best creations stand out. What good is suffocated brilliance? Weed, weed. Tear out what does not advance you. A season of carelessness, and you will find weeds have taken hold, have put down strong taproots; it may take several seasons to control their growth. Constant weeding, however, decreases work. Weeds are easiest to control when they are small and rootless. Weed, weed.

151 ~ *You cannot control a puppet if you cannot find the strings.*

Anyone can serve your purposes, if you find the controlling strings. Before you attempt to get cooperation, observe your potential partners. Which ones are motivated by status, which by power, which by friendship? Offer them what they want. It does no good to offer something that has no value to the recipient: you lose something that might be of value to you, and you gain nothing. But when you have found the strings, you can make any puppet dance to your tune.

152 ~ *Give something to get something, but never give without getting.*

You are surrounded by desires and demands; you yourself are filled with desires and demands. Meeting others' desires, satisfying others' demands, will increase your power, but only if you remember to satisfy your own as well. Do not hesitate to ask something of someone who requests something of you. It will not benefit you to be a well from which all draw water but that has no source of replenishment.

153 ~ *Soft does not mean weak.*

Strong does not mean hard. It is possible to give and still be strong. It is possible to be gentle and still be competent. It is difficult to show vulnerability to those who are positioned to hurt us, but it is sometimes necessary. Do not be recklessly open, for that will certainly invite damage. But to attempt invulnerability is to court damage as well.

154 ~ *It will be neither the best nor the worst.*

The future is never exactly as you plan. It is either better or worse, sometimes slightly, sometimes greatly. Do not expend too much energy in projecting the specifics of the immediate future. Plan instead for the intermediate and distant future. Examine the patterns around you to determine how to respond to future opportunities. But do not try too fiercely to control tomorrow, for it always eludes you.

155 ~ *The city is only busy if you are from the country.*

Things may seem complex and confusing now. But that is only in comparison with your usual life. Imagine yourself at war, in a flood, in an earthquake; you will find that today's problems look mild by comparison. You may find that you can endure the complications in order to gain your end. Or you may find that you deeply yearn for a calmer, less conflicted life. Decide, then act accordingly.

156 ~ *Get some perspective.*

Imagine that you are on the moon, looking down at yourself. Imagine that you are a historian, looking back on yourself a hundred years hence. What do you see? How important are your worries from that perspective? It is important to be conscious of every moment, to value each moment as you live it. Beyond that, view everything from sufficient distance to gain perspective.

157 ~ *Keep trying; someone will finally say yes.*

Many fail because of lack of persistence. Many a great idea, a great project, has failed because its inventor, its author, lost faith in it. If you truly believe in something, keep asking. Keep asking, and someday someone will say yes to you. The real test of genius is not in the moment of creation, but in the months or even years it takes to gain a true hearing.

158 ~ *Pain is not necessarily gain.*

We can learn from pain, it is true. But it is also human instinct to avoid pain. Follow that instinct. If something hurts you, there is reason to avoid it. There is no reason to place yourself continually in the path of pain. You will be handed sufficient learning in life without seeking it. Avoid what hurts. Seek what gives you joy.

159 ~ *You are on the brink of true success.*

This is the time to move forward confidently. Remember that confidence convinces. You are close to what you want, what you yearn for. Move toward it vigorously. In moving, you will draw to yourself those who wish to move in your direction. Do not hesitate. Seek within yourself the strength to move, then strike out.

160 ~ *Remember who you are.*

Never forget who you are, or where your center is. Remember this: You are not your position. You are not your relationships. You are not your creations. You have, deep in yourself, a unique solidity. Permit yourself to yield to others. Permit yourself to bend. But never permit yourself to give away that essential truth that is you.

161 ~ *Let tomorrow worry about tomorrow.*

Concentrate on solving immediate problems, and long-range problems will diminish or evaporate. Nothing occurs that is not set in motion. Nothing stops without being halted. Put forth your energy into examining what you can do now, in this hour, to improve your condition. Then set about to do it, without hesitation and without fail.

162 ~ *There are oracles all around you; just listen.*

Each day brings you many messages of wisdom. Tune into them. The oracle may speak through others, or through books and music, art and nature. You must be listening always for the advice that shows you the way. There is nothing in this world that does not speak. If a flower does not speak, it is because you are not listening. If a stone seems dumb, it is because you lack ears attuned to it.

163 ~ *A modest exterior may hide beauty; an extravagant facade may hide rot.*

Do not rely upon appearances only in making judgments. The person who so impresses you now may later be revealed as shallow or deceitful. The person who seems plain, uninteresting, may be the one to whom you turn in moments of difficulty. Learn to distinguish true quality in people. There is a solidity to real talent, real love, real worth that rings true. Learn to attend to its bell, to its resonant vibration.

164 ~ *Attend to the moment.*

Living in the past, living in the future have the same effect: they divorce you from the simple present in which you truly exist. Spend little time regretting the past or congratulating yourself on it; spend time judiciously in planning for the future, but do not attempt to foresee it in exact detail. Instead, attend to your present tasks. What should you be doing at this moment? It is in the present that past and future intersect. Proper action in the moment eliminates repetition of past mistakes and builds a happier future.

165 ~ *Use a sword when appropriate; use a dagger when necessary.*

There is a weapon for every battle. Sometimes you will need the broad blade of a sword to cut through to your goal; sometimes you need the sharp point of a dagger. If you are having difficulty, it may be because you have selected the wrong weapon for the battle in which you are engaged. Examine your opponents well. Ask yourself what will work to gain your objective. Then look to your armory and select appropriately.

166 ~ *Nothing is ever truly finished.*

Not only does the present have roots in the past, but it puts forth branches into the future. We struggle constantly to finish things. But in the completion of one project is the genesis of the next. In the preparation of one program is the seed of the next. Do not become disheartened if each task seems to spawn six more. That is the nature of growth.

167 ~ *Actions are words. Words are also words.*

You are communicating constantly, with everything you say and do. You may believe that you hide your real intention, but others notice the slight arch of your brow, the slight twist of your lip. There is no way to completely monitor all your communications. All you can hope for is this: that you learn to know yourself so well that nothing about you takes you by surprise. Know always what you are saying, and mean it.

168 ~ *Know when to rest; know when to stop.*

Do not try to keep pressing ahead when you have become tired or others have become intransigent. Pull back and examine the situation more coolly. Perhaps it is time to give up, to realize that your objective cannot be met at this time. Perhaps it is time for a brief rest, one that will revive you and permit you to move forward more energetically later. Or perhaps it is time to admit defeat. Never allow yourself to give up prematurely. However, you must draw back sufficiently to decide what is the best course of action.

169 ~ *The cost is never too high for what you really want.*

If you really want something, no cost is ever too much. When you find something too costly, do not tell yourself that you are too poor to afford it. Tell yourself, rather, I am unwilling to pay that price for that success, for that advancement, for that honor. You will no longer be someone who cannot afford what you want; you become someone who refuses to pay for what is not needed, not sufficiently desired. But when you have found what you really cherish, be willing to pay whatever price you must pay.

170 ~ *Look down and around, as well as up.*

You never know whence help will come. You never know whence trouble will come. Do not look only up; do not look only down; do not look only around. Do not distinguish people by their status in relation to you, for someone far beneath you can as easily cause you hurt or gain as someone far above you. Be aware of everyone around you, at all times.

171 ~ *Circles and spheres, not lines and cubes.*

The horizon looks like a straight line, but it is in reality a vast circle. And that vast circle is again only an illusion, for the earth is really a sphere, a three-dimensional circle. Similarly, your life may look like a straight line, moving toward a goal. But all life spirals and circles; it does not move directly forward. Accept the circling nature of life. Work with it, rather than against it.

172 ~ *If you feel out of place, perhaps you should find another.*

When you feel yourself out of place, you may need to make changes to fit better into your surroundings. You may need to change clothes to fit an occasion; you may need to alter your speech to be heard. But always calculate the cost to yourself for making such changes. Compromise is useful, but not always good. Neither resist compromise because you hold too fast to your own ways, nor yield too quickly and lose your identity. Yield, but only when you are able to maintain your center. Compromise, but only when you gain more than you lose.

173 ~ *Where there is smoke, there is a smoker.*

Do not deceive yourself about the meaning of the difficulties you have been facing. Difficulties are caused by people. That person could be you: make certain that you are not sending smoke signals to yourself. But if you are certain that you are not the cause of the problems you face, look around you. Who stands to gain from your difficulty? It may be someone who is usually an enemy to you; it could be someone you think of as a friend. Examine the situation carefully to determine who is behind the smoke screen.

174 ~ *When in Rome, drink red wine; when in England, strong tea.*

You must adapt to your surroundings; do not expect them to adapt to you. And do not expect your surroundings to be unchanging. Your job is to observe carefully and constantly. You are a traveler, an explorer. You are always crossing borders into new territory. Do not imagine that back-home ways are always the best. The best is the way that works in the land where you live.

175 ~ *There is no shame in not knowing what to do.*

If you do not know something, admit you do not know. If you do not know what to do next, ask for help and advice. More trouble is caused by those who refuse to admit their limitations than by those who do. More trouble is given to those who do not admit what they do not know than to those who do. You cannot know everything. You cannot do everything. Ask for help.

176 ~ *Just because you can do something, do not think you must.*

Ability becomes liability when you forget how to say no. If you are skilled or talented at something, others will expect you to perform constantly, even when you are not interested, prepared, or ready. Remember the power of no; it must be you who decides when a talent is used, when it is withheld. If you have agreed to perform, do so wholeheartedly. If you are merely expected to perform, determine whether there is sufficient gain for you to do so.

177 ~ *Eat what nourishes you.*

We need what we need. There is no benefit to ignoring your needs. Needs do not go away when they are unmet; they simply remain, unmet, forming a great pool of craving. You need what you need. Find what satisfies your hungers. Do not believe your needs are too huge or too extreme to be met. Every hunger can be sated, every thirst quenched. Seek until you find.

178 ~ *Discover where the power really lies.*

There is power around you. Some of it is available to you. You must study carefully to determine where power resides. Do not let the trappings of power fool you, for they sometimes hide the timid and the powerless. Power reveals itself as clarity, as intelligence, as confidence. Power is only energy. Find it and become its friend.

179 ~ *Take a deep breath and jump.*

When you are on the edge, you can either jump or be pushed. Retreat is not an option. You come to the edge because you yearn to move, to be moved. You come to the edge because stasis is no longer as important as movement. Accept that you have arrived at your present position because you moved in this direction. Accept that, and accept as well your desire to move forward. The times do not call for timidity and caution. Move aggressively to attain your desire.

180 ~ *Pay what you owe. Do not pay what you do not owe.*

It is vital that you keep your accounts clear. Do not allow debts to pile up unpaid. Pay them off, and do not incautiously acquire others. But do not pay more than you owe. Debts, whether of the monetary or the personal kind, can be falsely presented so that you appear to be more greatly in debt than you are. It is to your advantage to know at all times what you owe, and to whom.

181 ~ *Goodwill turns easily to rancor; rancor rarely turns to goodwill.*

Do not rely overmuch on goodwill. Matters change between people. Lovers part, relatives argue, associates dispute. When you rely upon goodwill to cement your agreements, you leave yourself vulnerable to changes of fortune with every change of relationship. No matter how confident you feel about another, be cautious in all dealings. Should nothing change, you will have lost nothing; should feelings change, you will be glad you protected yourself.

182 ~ *The clock does not control time.*

Time is endless. Infinity surrounds us. This is the truth. The clock is not the truth. The clock is not time. Time is that river in which we immerse ourselves, that wind in which we stand. Time is not seconds, minutes, hours. Do not let the clock dictate to you. Do not let the clock limit you. You have as much time as you need. You have as much time as there is.

183 ~ *In foolishness is deep wisdom; in play is the finest work.*

True success does not come from hard, serious work alone. You will become respected through such effort, but you will not gain acclaim. It is when you let the fool within you speak, the child play, that you rise above your peers. Find ways to play and ways to be foolish if you wish to be both happy and successful.

184 ~ *All words are poems. All poems are spells.*

We define our reality by the words we use to express it. Whatever words you use most frequently make up the song to which your life dances. When your talk is always of conflict and dispute, you will discover your life filled with difficulty. When your speech is full of hope, you will find hope. Words are power. Do not use them carelessly.

185 ~ *The hourglass has almost run through.*

The sands of time fall steadily, without ceasing, each grain exactly as valuable as the last grain, as the next. How have you used each irreplaceable moment of this day? Does each moment draw you closer to happiness, to freedom, to self-fulfillment? If not, what are you doing? How can you have forgotten how close you are, how close each of us is, to the end of our time? Linger in this moment, and consider how best to use the next.

186 ~ *You cannot become successful doing what you hate.*

Do not imagine that you can become truly successful doing something halfheartedly. Oh, you may make a minor stir; you may attract some minor notice. But real success comes to those who do what they passionately love. Notice the difference in those around you. There are those who perform competently, adequately. They become comfortable, but they are never successful. Then there are those in whom passion flames, who care deeply about everything they do. They attract attention: sometimes negative, often positive. It is they who truly succeed in the end.

187 ~ *The skills of the potter are not useless to the blacksmith.*

No skill is ever useless. There will be some things at which you excel, for which you can become renowned; certainly these are the skills you should polish and that you should seek to practice constantly. Other skills will come less easily to you; even with practice you may still remain awkward at their performance. But do not slight the learning of any skill. Take advantage of every opportunity to learn that life presents you. You cannot know what skills you will need in the future.

188 ~ *The fool is not the king's opposite; the fool is king in another realm.*

Success is finding your right place and recognizing it once you have found it. When you have found your place, you will be accorded respect; when you are out of place, you will be found foolish or inept. The treatment others accord you shows you whether you are properly placed or not. Do not rage if you have not succeeded sufficiently. Find a place where you can do so.

189 ~ *The doorway is part of the wall.*

Opportunity often appears as part of the run of things. It is easily overlooked, for it does not stand apart or call attention to itself. What seems to be an obstacle, a limitation, contains within it the opportunity you want. Look carefully at that wall. Study it until it reveals its openings to you. The best opening goes through, not around, the limitations and challenges you perceive.

190 ~ *Whipping the mule is as much work as the work itself.*

Wherever there is resistance, there is a reason for the resistance. If you must whip yourself into action, if you do not willingly go to a task, examine the causes of your unwillingness and your inaction. Flogging yourself into action consumes energy, energy that is then unavailable for the task. Those who achieve do so because they apply themselves enthusiastically. What is it you resist doing, and why?

191 ~ *The board is the same whether the game is chess or checkers.*

You do not determine the rules unless you are the one who initiates the game. Therefore, whenever possible, be the one who sets the pieces on the board. Select the game at which you are most adept; do not select a game according to the comfort and skill of your opponent. But when you enter a game already in progress, remember that you cannot win if you play a different game than your opponent. Do not make a single move until you have determined the game's rules and what pieces are in play.

192 ~ *The tree needs both water and minerals; the taproot finds both.*

Your deepest angers and your individual genius have the same root. Do not deny your shadow. Where there is a shadow, there is also bright light. Embrace that within you which you have denied. You are not perfect; no human is, or was meant to be. There is energy in anger. There is even thwarted energy in pain. Recognize this, and you can become whole.

193 ~ *Be certain the hero role is vacant before you audition for it.*

When the actors assemble, few yearn for supporting roles. Everyone dreams of being the hero. But though there are many supporting characters, there can be only one leading actor. If that role is taken, you must play a lesser one or leave the play, perhaps even leave the theater. Be careful when you find a clamoring within for a greater role. Rarely is there a play in which the hero has not already been cast. Try to take that role from the assigned player, and you will become the villain.

194 ~ *Before every gate, there is a guardian.*

Do not be discouraged when entry to a higher stage, a better life, becomes difficult. At every gate stands a guardian who discourages the timid and the halfhearted from entering. The guardian appears to say, "Do not enter." If you can hear the message fully, however, you will know that the guardian says, "Do not enter until you have . . . " or "Do not enter unless you are willing to . . . " Find out what the guardian requires. Then determine whether entry is worth the price to you.

195 ~ *Desire is no guarantee of satisfaction, but lack of desire is a guarantee of failure.*

It is good to want. Only those who want have the energy to reach. Only those filled with desire will move forward to attain their goal. But desire itself does not guarantee its satisfaction. The world does not owe you what you want. It is possible that you may not attain your goals. It is possible you may fail. But without wanting, you are certain to fall short. Without desire, you are certain to live hungry.

196 ~ *When a thing recurs, it is because you must learn a lesson.*

Watch for patterns in your life. When something happens over and over again, do not blame others, or fate, or bad luck. Examine instead what lesson you have resisted learning. That lesson keeps presenting itself to you and will do so until you learn it thoroughly. You have drawn this lesson to yourself for a reason. You are a magnet for this circumstance, this recurrent problem. Instead of complaining, be humble and learn. When the lesson is finally learned, the problem will dissolve.

197 ~ *Everything grows from something.*

With each moment, you are creating the future. You can plant unwittingly or deliberately, but plant you will. Do not try to control the future; control instead the present.

Within your hand you have a choice of harvests. If you wish grass, do not plant an elm. If you wish roses, do not plant peas. The most successful person is the one who recognizes each seed before it is planted and plants what he or she wishes to harvest.

198 ~ *Light and dark are not opposites.*

Be careful not to imagine opposition where there is none. Light and darkness are part of the same cosmos. They flow into each other. Look around you; even in light there is shadow, even in the deep night there are stars. Just so your life: Where you sense opposition, there is also connection. Where you sense struggle, there is a bond. Where you sense difference, there is identity.

199 ~ *You have come to the end of the road.*

Whatever you intended when you began this journey, you have come to this place, and so this is the place to which your journey was leading. What decisions have taken you here? Ask yourself what steps, what routes, took you here. Do not deny that you have been the traveler. Do not pretend that each step has not been yours. There will be more journey ahead, but you cannot move forward successfully until you understand how you arrived at this place.

200 ~ *Endings are more difficult than beginnings.*

Just as death is more difficult than birth, so any ending is more difficult than any beginning. We cling to what we know. We resist moving on. We fear the unknown future. So we slow down and procrastinate, or we rush forward and end matters precipitously. Neither benefits you. Endings come as a natural course. You need only notice and cooperate. Neither resist nor press too aggressively forward. And remember that beyond the ending is a new beginning.